Mosaic

Elle Junia

 BookLeaf Publishing

Presentation by *BookLeaf Publishing*

Web: www.bookleafpub.com

E-mail: info@bookleafpub.com

ISBN: 978-93-95755-92-4

First edition 2022

Dedication

For anyone and everyone who wants to make sense of it all.

Acknowledgement

The theme of this poetry collection came from a lot of personal reflection in a time of great personal challenge. To everyone who supported me, in big ways and small, thank you.

Shattered

Shattered
All the most beautiful things are
A stained glass mosaic
A once young, trusting heart.

Try to stay in one piece
You won't get very far
Our lives are a mosaic
Every piece leaves a scar.

Best Friends

A piece of your heart
And a piece of mine
Now, always and forever
They'll exist side by side.

A pair for your mosaic
And the pair that's now in mine
Makes a bright yellow sun
That I believe will always shine.

The world seems brighter when I'm with you
As I linger on the sun that we've made
Each day we make more memories together
With you there is no such thing as pain.

The sun cannot set when you're on it
And we have made this one our home.
Once two, now we're one forever
Our sun will shine even when we're grown.

Creation (Part 1)

When you're young, the world is full of magic
You see it and know you're magic too.
So you run around, a happy creator
You decide that your sky will be blue.

As a child, your feet are always calloused
Run through rocks and you won't feel a thing.
So you jump from shattered piece to piece creating
The grass will be green and full of twigs.

Everything seems brighter when you're younger
The colours, experience and scents.
To capture it, you put flowers all over
Vibrant blues and purples and reds.

As a child, your energy is unending
And your story has only begun.
Every memory becoming a piece of you
Especially when you're just having fun.

Growing Pains

The sun can't shine forever
Even the brightest stars fade
I should have known from the start
We would grow apart someday.

As we got older it was harder to linger here
Our paths led us separate ways
It was time to explore some new places
As much as we wanted to stay.

When I jumped from our sun for the last time
The edge cut my leg and it bled.
I don't remember change hurting so much
The development filled me with dread.

The question before me was this;
Where do I go from here?
What comfort is there after losing
The one place I had held so dear?

And I felt, for the first time
There was nowhere I belonged
Every edge cut the same
And every cut left me scarred.

Still I wandered through the glass
What other option did I have?
Until I could find somewhere to land
Something to replace what I once had.

Identity (Part 1)

Shattered
There was never just one piece of me.
I guess I knew it all along
But now it's much easier to see.

Whatever people know about me
It's only just a part
One piece of my identity
One fraction of a larger heart.

But you would think I could see the bigger
picture
Surely I could put it all together!
But I too see shattered pieces
Pieces I just can't seem to tether.

My identity should be a puzzle
Each part clicking into the whole
But instead it's a senseless junk drawer
And I'm supposed to be in control.

Shattered
I know who I am, yet I don't.
I see pieces, like every outsider
They should go together, but they won't.

Perspective (Part 1)

How different things look
When you land on a new colour.
How quickly things change
At the end of the summer.

When the bright golden sun
Seems duller, more gray
And all the things on earth
Are less vibrant just the same.

On the ground, that's where I am
This new perspective is shaded and richer.
Living amongst the deep green grass
Gives me an entirely new picture.

What once seemed so light and breezy
Is now heavy and tinted, more dark.
What I once saw as perfect and exciting
Appears broken, the image is stark.

For the first time, I feel I see the truth-
The intention behind the invention.
And everything seems purposeful now
It spreads like a bittersweet infection.

All at once it's mechanical and unexciting
Yet I feel a sense of enlightenment erupt.
Life is beautiful and disappointing in measure
Is this what it means to grow up?

Once I was…

Once I was young
And everything was fun
I didn't have a care in the world.
Now that I'm older
I'm begging the sun
To cleanse me of the things I have learned.

Once it was easy
To do all my chores
Then go back to playing the the grass.
Now it's much harder
To go from working long hours
To finding some time to relax.

Once I was riding
My bike down the road
I fell and cut open my knee.
My dad came out running
Fixed it up, held me close
And helped me to dry up my tears.

Now I am crying
From the internal pain
Of stress that never seems to end.
I wipe my own tears
Try to heal my own brain
On myself I must now depend.

Once my whole life
Was about what I loved
Passion was all I would chase.
Now I barely have time
And those passions are shrugged
I call them hobbies and they take up no space.

Rose

I had started working on the flowers
The day I met you.
When I saw you for the first time
It was something new.

It was like my whole like
Was seen through that rose coloured hue
So I felt very optimistic
I wanted to get to know you.

You joined me in the garden
Helped me create all the petals
Until my mosaic was full
Of bright pinks and oranges and yellows.

When I looked into the future with you
I saw only good things to come.
When I looked at the present, too
It seemed even brighter than the sun.

I ran with you through the roses
My feet finally calloused once more.
I could only see the petals
And I couldn't feel the thorns.

Shadows

Even on the brightest days
The shadows must remain.

Sometimes we are covered by them
Other times their presence fades.

Most days we wish them away
Believing they will leave a stain.

But sometimes their cool dark touch
Protects us from greater pain.

At first the shadows scared me
When I was broken, I entered afraid.

But as I stayed I realized the healing
Hidden in the shadow's embrace.

Sometimes the darkness teaches us
Lessons we've no other way to gain.

And in the quiet, empty darkness
Only our truths can reign.

Resilience

It doesn't get any less painful
My skin doesn't get any tougher
Maybe it's something in my soul.

It tells me to keep going
Because every new scratch
Makes my life a little more full.

Moving on
Feels like a loss
But really, it's making me whole.

I press on through the pain
And with each step I take
I can feel a new, stronger pull.

The pull overcomes
All the pain that I face
I feel both more and less in control.

I am strong and I am free
But even more than these
I don't fear what I've yet to endure.

It doesn't get any less painful
But now I have strength and direction
That comes from deep growth in my soul.

So I pick myself up
And I search for the pieces
So one day I feel truly full.

Creation (Part 2)

It's harder when you're older
To see the fun in creating your world
Because for everything you're choosing
There's something you're letting go.

Picking and choosing
Nothing comes from thin air
And for each piece you hold onto
Another must disappear.

The past may stay in your mosaic
But each time you chase a new start
What you see before you is so different
You feel you've torn everything apart.

It may break your heart
But as the pieces come together
Nostalgia will be overwhelmed
In the face of something better.

Things will never be as they were
Creation is destruction, in a way
Yet there's beauty in each new creation
Once you see it, it will never go away.

Identity (Part 2)

It was never going to be a puzzle.
Why?
Because puzzles are perfect.
And what am I?
A person.

My pieces don't fit perfectly
They weren't made for one another.
I am a mess of all the things
That influenced me
That created me
That defined me.
I am a collection
Of people
Places
Moments
Memories
Multiple identities I met along the way.

I feel broken
Yet I'm not
This is how I was supposed to be;
A thousand broken pieces that tell a story.
Side by side, but not intertwined.

A person is not just one thing
A puzzle only shows you one picture
I am not just one thing
I'm different things to different people
There are many pictures that tell a story.

And there are angles to this story.
While each piece complete the whole,
It's quite messy.
There are few compliments
Only chaotic energy.

How could a puzzle capture my essence?
Shattered pieces are a better tribute.
Glimpses of every piece that makes me whole
Including the holes and sharp edges.
Changing colours of moments that passed.

I am pieces that don't always make sense.
Yet I'm still very proud to say
They are me in every single way.
My confusion and my pain
Over the edges that sometimes cut deep
They're not wrong things to feel
They're a part of my mosaic
The gorgeous mess that I've made.

Scars

I stopped long enough to see them
Paused, just long enough to feel them
All of the scars I've gained
For every time I've chosen change.

For a moment, I was discouraged
As I examined my body, so wounded
All at once I felt the pain I'd been hiding
Each mark was felt at once, it was binding.

I couldn't believe it looked so bad
There seemed no end to the scars that I had
I wanted to hide, but then
It all started to click inside my head.

These scars aren't blemishes- they're decorations
Proud proof of my many creations
Each one telling stories of the moments
I abandoned fear and pressed on with devotion.

Why keep a medal in a drawer?
Why pretend not to keep score?
When the evidence of greatness is right there
It's okay to take a moment to stare.

I'll proud of the bruises and bumps
Let them remind me of the many jumps
Knowing the picture in the end
Will be better for each wound I have to mend.

Perspective (Part 2)

How easy it is
To be lost in a moment
Myself, I've been lost in so many.

Each one looks a little different
And that's how I know
Know to cherish it
To watch it pass, eyes wide open.

The feeling will never come again-
Except, maybe, in the most vivid memory
So I must appreciate the perspective
While I have it.

It's not just the seasons
But each one has a haze
A way to experience it as it's meant to be
A way to touch the past
While I remain beneath that haze
For a distanced visit
That lasts only a little while.

It's not just the emotions
But each one affects my perspective
Casting its own vague shadow
On the events that will come to pass.

It's not just time or maturity
Though I see things differently now than I did
then.

What a gift it is
The experience of new perspectives
New perceptions of an ordinary thing.
To see colours I've never seen
Cause feelings I've never felt
And may never feel again.

Reflection

Suddenly, I saw it all with clarity
The way this life thing works
All at once it all made sense
I finally understood the purpose.

Your life is a mosaic
Your story, a stained glass picture
And there's a reason it's in pieces
A reason there are so many colours.

You make it as you go along
Each piece is a part of your story
A memory, an interest, chosen family
Anything that becomes part of your identity.

And you linger on each piece for a while
Some a long time, some only a few minutes
Your life is coloured by the moments you live in
And their colours envelop your vision.

When change comes and you must move on
The edges of the glass are quite sharp
It hurts to move on, this you know
The pain is felt also when you restart.

Still you add on and on to your mosaic
Not always seeing what you're working towards
But each piece is important and special
Of this you couldn't be more sure.

And this mosaic will be a true reflection
Though you can't always see what others can
It is truer than a face in a mirror
And it will all come together in the end.

The Bigger Picture

And I wonder what it looks like
From the outside looking in
For I know others see it much differently.

Each person I meet takes the pieces of me
The ones they know, and puts them together
They form an opinion- an understanding of who
I am
And they see a bigger picture.

But each person has different pieces
And they put them together differently in their
minds
So every person has a different picture.

And none of them are wrong
But none of them are true
For a segment says little about the whole.

Still, they see a bigger picture than I can usually
see
From the inside looking out
Within the mess, it's hard to understand the
message.

As for me, it's quite blurry
As though the image is just out of focus
And I'm right there, on the cusp of
understanding
Almost seeing the true picture
Almost knowing how to interpret the pieces.

A Thousand Lives

But it didn't have to go just this way
And my mosaic could look quite different today
If any of the choices I made
Had been made in a different way.

I don't think of paths converging
Or stepping stones that make the person I'm
becoming
I see each choice as a preview of one
Of the thousands of lives I could be exploring.

There were many different versions I could be
And each one would be equally me
If I had done even one thing differently
There would have been a new life to see.

I got a taste of each one
For a brief moment, that life had begun
Then one choice began another one
And that one was over and done.

Some say their lives have different chapters
But for me it's a much larger matter
Thousand of lives make up the one I've chased
after
In my mind, all the options remain plastered.

I wonder what each one would be like
What choices would make up those lives
There's a wisdom I feel, a wider sight
I see the beauty each adds to this life.

It's exhausting, yet empowering
At times, quite inspiring
To wonder about the lives I could be missing
Yet feel grateful for the one I am now living.
Hoping
It's the best one that could be occurring.

Mosaic(s)

The true beauty of life
Is that it isn't ours alone
Our story is a small part
Of a bigger one we create
With those we love.

For our mosaics have ties
To every life that has impacted ours
Whether they grow together
Or apart
If it's only one piece connecting
Or many
Still, there's a larger piece of art.

I think of my family
How ours have been connected since my birth.
They must be side by side
Every step of the way.

Then I think if the way
My love's and mine have grown together.
Since the moment we met
They've grown closer and closer
Until
There are almost no separations

Like two sides of a waterfall
Together we flow
Only drops of mist
That go in new directions.

And the image gets bigger
As I think of more and more people
How they connect to me as well as others.

My heart just soars
Imagining what they all look like together
Messy in the most beautiful way
Nonsensical but connected all the same.

And as grand as I imagined my image to be
When I imagine it as part of something more
It seems much more wonderful to think of it
As a unique patch filling one part of the whole.

Where it ends
I don't know
Maybe it never does
I've never felt more connected
To anything more beautiful.

Finer Details

I imagine the big moments
Relationships, things I've been involved in
As large pieces
Ones that complete a foundational part of the
picture.

I imagine that the most important parts of me
Can be most easily seen
For they're integral
And draw your eyes immediately.

But there is more to my scene than the
foundation
There are subtleties and small, finer details
For a great tree is nothing without leaves
And the sky seems so bland without stars.

I feel my foundation is solid
So I focus on those finer details
Chasing the things that matter most
I focus on spending more time with them
Adding character to a cookie-cutter shape.

More moments with my hobbies
More product to showcase my passion
Improvement- goals met I'd only dreamed of
Like a medal to adorn my canvas.

More memories made with those I love
Embellishing those pieces we share
The images become more realistic
With every new feature that's engraved.

Life is made of these details -
It's the little things that make good things last.

The Light

A stained glass mosaic
Is nothing but shattered glass
A lucky, mismatched pattern
Until the light hits it.

Only when the light
Illuminates the picture
Does its beauty shine bright.

And I can see the light coming through
Projecting my mosaic onto the empty floor
below
The colours, which are separate on the ground
Mingle together in the air
Creating the most unique haze
A colour never seen before
My essence, never to be replicated again.

The colour is who I am
I feel a completeness in my soul as I take it in
Peace, clarity.
As the colour envelops me
Whispers to me
Explains, wordlessly, who I am.

The image itself
The reflection of it on the floor
Although duller than the real thing
Is so vibrant and complex
It might take an eternity to absorb it all
Even longer to examine it fully.

As the light comes in
I stand on the floor
Analyzing the effect.
All at once
My whole life is here, before my eyes
And it is wonderful beyond words.

The Final Picture

It isn't just one picture
One scene
Not one focused depiction with endless detail
It's rather like seeing everything all at once.

As if a movie
Or the entirety of the world
Was put together in one piece
Every place
Every image
Together, to be taken in all at once.

Somehow,
I see it all.
From a distance-
Far enough that nothing is beyond my field of
vision
And yet every single detail is clear and vivid.

I can see the whole
As well as I see the moments
The sun
As clearly as the shadows
Each droplet
On a delicate petal

Is as eye-catching
As the flower itself
The waterfall
Is seen alongside the desert
And somehow, it makes perfect sense.

The thousands of lives are seen
And the beginnings aren't the only parts seen
There are moments
Each life had the potential to reoccur
Many opportunities
To go a different way
Are represented here
In crossroads
And I see how all the lives were connected
How their unique hazes appear in many places
And my life is a collection
Inspired by them all.

Everything fits
And everything has a purpose
And that which once felt wretched
Has been made beautiful
That which was dark
Only filters the light
Creating a new way for it to be
A new shade through which it is seen.

And all of the colours
With their individual meanings and significance
Stand alone
And yet reveal and embellish one another
Together, they are complete
And the simple mysteries
Are revealed in one another
And the final picture
Reveals every mystery
Declaring, once and for all;

There was beauty
In every single moment
For all of the most beautiful things
Are shattered.